No
Museu

D0594032

GREAT PLAINS

NATIVE

NATIONS

VOLUME III

EDWARD S.
CURTIS

GREAT PLAINS

Christopher Cardozo

PRODUCED BY CALLAWAY EDITIONS

A BULFINCH PRESS BOOK
LITTLE, BROWN AND COMPANY
Boston · New York · Toronto · London

First Edition

(COVER)
THE BLACKFOOT COUNTRY, 1926

(FRONTISPIECE)
A CHILD'S LODGE – PIEGAN, 1910

ISBN 0-8212-2358-5

Library of Congress Catalog Card Number 96-76728

Bulfinch Press is an imprint and trademark of Little, Brown and Company (Inc.)
Published simultaneously in Canada by Little, Brown & Company (Canada) Limited

PRINTED IN HONG KONG

TABLE OF CONTENTS

PREFACE

Edward Sheriff Curtis took more than 40,000 photographs of over eighty tribal groups throughout the western United States, Canada, and Alaska for his twenty-volume, twenty-portfolio magnum opus, The North American Indian, *published from 1907 to 1930. He had a particular interest, however, in the native nations of the Great Plains. Four of the first six volumes and accompanying portfolios were devoted exclusively to Plains tribes.*

The native peoples of the Great Plains were semi-nomadic hunter-gatherers whose culture and way of life revolved around the availability of game, most dramatically the buffalo. These societies prized strength, self-reliance and a profound interdependence with nature. Curtis was fascinated with these proud, fiercely independent peoples, their highly developed material culture, and their rich, multi-layered religious and spiritual lives

Curtis focused on many aspects of life on the Plains. While his intention was to present as comprehensive a picture of Indian life as possible, it was his landscapes, portraits, and images of rituals and ceremonies that were at the heart of his original publications. The extraordinary diversity of people, places, and cultures that Curtis came into contact with provided him with an especially rich palette.

His Plains portraits, especially those of tribal leaders, are among his most famous images. As an artist, Curtis was drawn to the powerful faces of the Plains Indians. Their striking cheekbones and strongly etched features worked well with Curtis's dramatic portraiture style, allowing him to make full use of the dramatic lighting and graphic compositions of which he was so fond. After tremendous initial distrust, once the tribes were acquainted with Curtis and understood his mission, they came to trust him, actively soliciting him to photograph them. They realized that if an accurate, sympathetic record was to be preserved for posterity, particularly for their own descendants, Curtis was the only photographer capable of accomplishing this task in a sensitive, respectful manner.

The landscapes Curtis encountered, with rivers, rolling hills, valleys, verdant plains, forests, and the Badlands, also inspired his artistic sensibility. His images taken during winter of Northern Plains peoples such as the Sioux and Apsaroke represent the degree to which Curtis was devoted to his life's work and to its exhaustive portrayal of tribal life. Travel and photography, even during the summer months, was arduous and difficult; during winter months it was nearly impossible. Few photographers ever went through the hardships necessary to make such photographs. The winter images Curtis created are not only unusual, but also uncommonly serene and beautiful.

The ceremonies, religion, and mythology of the Plains peoples were also of great importance to Curtis. He took numerous photographs, made many wax-cylinder recordings, and wrote extensive text about these rapidly disappearing rites and beliefs. Curtis was given access to sacred aspects of Plains life that had been revealed to no other white man. He succeeded in creating an unparalleled record that is still valued today. — c.c.

(OPPOSITE)

THE EAGLE-CATCHER, 1908

By neighboring tribes the Hidatsa were considered as very skilful in capturing eagles. Their method was the not unusual one of going to some high hill or mountain-top and digging a hole in the ground sufficiently large for a man to conceal himself therein with comfort. This was covered loosely with brush on which a bait of meat was laid. As an eagle alighted a bronzed arm slipped swiftly through the brush and seized the bird by the legs. The first captive was tethered as a decoy, and then as eagle after eagle lit they were caught in turn and choked to death with a rawhide rope. If a bird fought for freedom and fastened its talons in the hunter's wrist, he knew where to press the tendons of its legs to compel it to release its hold.

Being the largest as well as the most majestic of birds, the eagle was greatly venerated, and trapping him was attended with much supplication, that the eagle spirits might not be offended by the taking of their bodies. Volume IV, pages 136-137.

(OVERLEAF)

PIEGAN ENCAMPMENT, 1900

The picture not only presents a characteristic view of an Indian camp on an uneventful day, but also emphasizes the grand picturesqueness of the environment of the Piegan, living as they do almost under the shadow of the towering Rocky mountains. Folio plate 207, Volume VI.

THE MEDICINE-MAN, 1907

Invocation and supplication enter so much into the life of the Indian that this picture of the grim old warrior invoking the Mysteries is most characteristic. The subject . . . is Slow Bull. Folio plate 76, Volume III.

Slow Bull . . . Ogalala. Born 1844. First war-party at fourteen, under Red Cloud, against Apsaroke. Engaged in fifty-five battles with Apsaroke, Shoshoni, Ute, Pawnee, Blackfeet, and Kutenai. Struck seven first coups. At seventeen he captured one hundred and seventy horses from Apsaroke. In the same year he received medicine from buffalo in a dream while he slept on a hilltop, not fasting, but resting from travel on the war-path. Counted two honors in one fight, when the Lakota charged an Apsaroke camp and were routed. Slow Bull returned to the enemy; his horse stepped into a hole and fell, and an Apsaroke leaped on him. He threw his antagonist off, jumped on his horse, and struck his enemy in the face with his bow. At that moment another Apsaroke dashed up and dealt him a glancing blow in the back with a hatchet. Slow Bull counted coup on him also. He has been a subchief of the Ogalala since 1878. Volume III, page 189.

A PIEGAN DANDY, 1900

The Piegan, Cheyenne, and Arapaho belong to the western division of the Algonquian linguistic family. Geographically the Piegan are rather widely separated from the others. Each tribe of the trio has planted its name firmly in the literature and history of the northern plains.

The Piegan, with the kindred Blackfeet and Bloods, were a vigorous people, roaming over a vast territory, half in the United States and half in British America. Being noted hunters with great quantities of furs and hides for barter, their territory was an important one to traders. Volume VI, page xi.

THE LAND OF THE ATSINA, 1908

The Atsina, commonly designated Gros Ventres of the Prairie, are of the Algonquian stock and a branch of the Arapaho. . . .

In the days of the early fur-traders the tribe was known as Fall Indians, Gens de Rapides, *from the fact that when first seen they dwelt at the falls of the Saskatchewan.* Volume V, page 103.

THE GRIZZLY-BEAR – PIEGAN, 1911

Men wrapped in buffalo-robes . . . wearing a broad belt of grizzly-bear fur and having grizzly-bear claws around the biceps of each arm and around each calf, and on his head a pair of claws projecting upward and inward like buffalo-horns. . . . were Kyáyatsi, *Grizzly-bear Braves.* Volume VI, page 20.

DAUGHTER OF AMERICAN HORSE, 1908

The dress of the women consisted of a garment made of finely tanned deerskins, which extended from the shoulders to midway of the knee and ankle. Sleeves reaching nearly to the wrist were tied at intervals on the under side. . . . The sides of the dress were sewn from armpits to bottom. A dress regarded as well-made was fringed at its bottom and sleeves, and finely decorated at the shoulders and arms with porcupine quills, beads, and shells. Volume III, page 28.

(OPPOSITE)

MOTHER AND CHILD –
APSAROKE, 1908

In stature and vigor the Apsaroke, or Crows, excelled all other tribes of the Rocky Mountain region, and were surpassed by none in bravery and in devotion to the supernatural forces that gave them strength against their enemies. Social laws, rigidly adhered to, prevented marriage to those even distantly related, and the hardships of their life as hunters eliminated infant weaklings. The rigors of this life made the women as strong as the men; and women who could carry a quarter of a buffalo apparently without great exertion, ride all day and all night with a raiding war-party, or travel afoot two hundred and fifty miles across an unmarked wilderness of mountains, plains, and swollen streams in four days and nights, were not the women to bring forth puny offspring. Volume IV, page 3.

(OVERLEAF)

A PAINTED TIPI – ASSINIBOIN, 1926

A tipi painted with figures commemorative of a dream experienced by its owner is a venerated object. Its occupants enjoy good fortune, and there is no difficulty in finding a purchaser when after a few years the owner, according to custom, decides to dispose of it. Folio plate 633, Volume XVIII.

(OPPOSITE)

BLACK BELLY – CHEYENNE, 1927

The extreme age of this Cheyenne is quite apparent. Folio plate 671,
Volume XIX.

(OVERLEAF)

IN A PIEGAN LODGE, 1910

*Little Plume with his son Yellow Kidney occupies the position of honor,
the space at the rear opposite the entrance. The picture is full of
suggestion of the various Indian activities. In a prominent place lie the
ever-present pipe and its accessories on the tobacco cutting-board. From
the lodge-poles hang the buffalo-skin shield, the long medicine-bundle,
an eagle-wing fan, and deerskin articles for accoutering the horse. The
upper end of the rope is attached to the intersection of the lodge-poles,
and in stormy weather the lower end is made fast to a stake near the
centre of the floor space.* Folio plate 188, Volume VI.

(OPPOSITE)

BUFFALO-BERRY GATHERERS –
MANDAN, 1908

The women's dress consisted of two mountain-sheep skins sewn together down the sides and over the shoulders. . . . and the bottom was fringed and hung with small pieces of sheep-hoof. No embroidery ornamented the garment, which reached the ankles. Sleeves extended nearly to the wrists, and the upper part between the lines of fur was painted. . . .

    Staple foods were corn, beans, squash, sunflower seeds, and meat, principally that of the buffalo. . . . Choke-cherries, buffalo-berries, service-berries, turnips (pomme blanche)*, and wild tubers were gathered in quantity.* Volume V, pages 143, 144.

(OVERLEAF)

IN THE LAND OF THE SIOUX, 1905

This picture illustrates the general character of the Sioux country. The broad, rolling prairie is broken by low hills, while here and there lie pools of stagnant water in old buffalo-wallows. The subjects of the picture are Red Hawk, Crazy Thunder, and Holy Skin, three Ogalala. Folio plate 95, Volume III.

PLACATING THE SPIRIT OF A
SLAIN EAGLE – ASSINIBOIN, 1926

For their feathers, which were used in many ways as ornaments and as fetishes, eagles were caught by a hunter concealed in a brush-covered pit. A rather elaborate ceremony took place over the bodies of the slain birds for the purpose of placating the eagle spirits. Folio plate 634, Volume XVIII.

TRAVAUX – PIEGAN, 1900

With most of the plains tribes the travois was the universal vehicle for transporting camp equipment, but is now rarely seen. In the days before the acquisition of horses a smaller form of the same device was drawn by dogs. Folio plate 193, Volume VI.

FOUR HORNS – ARIKARA, 1908

Born in 1847 near Fort Berthold. At . . . fourteen he accompanied a war-party against the Sioux. Two years later he enlisted as scout at Fort Buford; he served also at Fort Phil. Kearny, where in a skirmish with Sioux he had a horse shot under him. Returning that summer to the village at Fort Berthold he led a party in pursuit of some Chippewa who had murdered a Hidatsa, and succeeded in killing two of them. Twice he joined in successful pursuit of Sioux horse-raiders. He fasted several times. On the third morning of his first fast three horse-skulls and a buffalo-skull were fastened with rawhide ropes to the muscles of his back. He dragged them a mile to the Hidatsa village, encircled it, and returned to the starting-point, but no vision was experienced. The following summer . . . his father . . . took him to the burial-ground and fastened him to a post by slits through his back-muscles. From sunset to sunrise he walked around the post, constantly pulling on the rope. The next year his father led him to the same place and had another man tie four horse-skulls and a buffalo-skull to his back, and these . . . became entangled in the roots of a stump and he had to free them without using his hands. During the Sun Dance of the succeeding year he was fastened, again by his father, to a resilient ash pole, which, springing back when he pulled on the ropes, greatly increased the torture. . . . but no vision was vouchsafed him. Volume V, page 179.

LITTLE HAWK – BRULÉ, 1907

This portrait exhibits the typical Brulé physiognomy. Folio plate 89, Volume III.

(OPPOSITE)

MOTHER AND CHILD, 1905

When a child was born, the parents prepared a feast and sent for a wichásha-waká^n, asking him to name the infant. The name bestowed was always one suggested by some animal or object seen during one of his fasts, and the accompanying prayer was one taught him during a vision. The Santee custom of giving to children fixed names depending on the order in which they were born did not prevail with the Teton. Volume III, page 18.

(OPPOSITE)

MEDICINE LODGE – APSAROKE, 1908

Not all men who had had visions were medicine-men, that is, healers. The medicine that was given to a man was more likely to be intended for his protection in battle and to give him good-fortune in his undertakings. If in his vision he saw a spirit effecting a cure, his medicine was known to be for healing and he was summoned by the ill for that purpose. He was Akbadhíu-mahpé, *He That Does Supernatural Things. Treatment was by singing, blowing, sucking, and other forms of conjuration. A man who could read the future, as well as cure disease, was* Biduhpák-mahpé, *Supernatural Person.* Volume IV, page 180.

(OVERLEAF)

THE PIEGAN, 1910

This scene on Two Medicine river near the eastern foot-hills of the Rocky mountains is typical of the western portion of the Piegan country, where the undulating upland prairies become rougher and more broken, and finally give place abruptly to mountains. Folio plate 184, Volume VI.

TEARING LODGE – PIEGAN, 1910

Pínokiminuksh is one of the few Piegans of advanced years and retentive memory. He was born about 1835 on Judith river in what is now northern Montana, and was found to be a valuable informant on many topics. The buffalo-skin cap is a part of his war costume, and was made and worn at the command of a spirit in a vision. Folio plate 187, Volume VI.

RED WING – APSAROKE, 1908

Born about 1858. Mountain Crow; Piegan Lodge clan; Lumpwood society. Obtaining no medicine by fasting, he purchased that of brown crane and owl, and led a successful war-party with it. Captured two guns in battle. When stationed at Fort Custer as United States scout he accompanied a detachment of troops in pursuit of Sioux horse-raiders; the latter surrendered, and Red Wing shook hands with one of them, subsequently claiming dákshe *since he had been the first to touch the enemy. A strict interpretation of the rules allowed the honor. Volume IV, page 204.*

(OPPOSITE)

SIOUX GIRL, 1907

A young Sioux woman in a dress made entirely of deerskin, embroidered with beads and porcupine-quills. Folio plate 97, Volume III.

(OVERLEAF)

ARIKARA MEDICINE CEREMONY – THE BEARS, 1908

As the entire fraternity danced, there was evident uneasiness and excitement, and constant watching of the entry-way. A warning shout was heard among the dancers as from the entrance dashed two or three men hotly pursued by two Bears. The dancers fled in every direction, pursued by the Bears, who skilfully simulated the actions of real animals. Even as the Bears chased the dancers, brave individuals tried to slip up behind and strike them with sticks. To succeed in this was regarded as a great deed, since it imparted some of the medicine strength of the Bear. After a time the Bears returned to the lodge as though it were their den, and the dancers crept stealthily up to the entrance, peeping in, but carefully listening for any movement. Suddenly there was a cry, and out rushed the Bears again, and so great was the apparent fright of the dancers that they fell over one another in their eagerness to escape. This incident was repeated thrice, and then forth came the Bears and two Buffalo, the latter also mimicking the actions of real animals. Four times they appeared together, and then a dancer slipped up and gave the pipe to one of the Bears. With apparent feeling and fear the Bear took a puff at the pipe and emitted a groan of anguish: his power was broken. Volume V, page 74.

"FOR STRENGTH AND VISIONS" –
APSAROKE, 1908

In the morning. . . . came the men who were going to fast in the expectation of finding medicine. Each one had a medicine-man, with whom he came to a post about twice as high as a tall man, which his friends had set up in the ground just after the building of the sun-lodge. These posts, forty or fifty of them, were in a circle around the lodge. . . . The medicine-man painted the dancer with white. . . . Each medicine-man cut the breasts of his votary, pushed and twisted the skewers under the flesh, and slipped two ropes over them. Putting his hands against the man's breast, he pushed him away three times, then threw him with all his strength. . . . This was all done at sunrise. . . .

On the outside the forty men tied to their posts . . . were looking from their medicine to the eagle's nest and the Sun, crying, "O, Sun, I do this for you!" and always pulling and falling back on their ropes, crying and praying for strength and visions. Volume IV, pages 77-78.

READY FOR *OKIPE* BUFFALO
DANCE – MANDAN, 1908

Men . . . participating in the eight Buffalo Dances to be performed on this day, were being painted by men of their own selection. As they stood with arms half outstretched at the sides, holding their bodies rigid and motionless by means of a staff in each hand, they were painted with a black stripe an inch and a half wide down the middle of the chest, which was then completely enclosed in black by a line drawn across it just below the clavicle, a second across the abdomen, and another down each side of the chest. The space thus circumscribed was painted red, but across the lower half ran three bars of white clay. The remainder of the upper part of the body was black, as were the neck, upper arms, wrists, hands, thighs, ankles, and feet. Forearms and calves were marked with longitudinal lines of alternate red and white. From a platform in the back of the lodge were taken the costumes of the Buffalo Dancers, each of whom now donned anklets of thick buffalo-hair, and a belt from which hung a knee-length kilt consisting of ribbons of buffalo-skin. A short buffalo-robe was thrown over the dancer's back and head, the long black hair falling over his face and leaving only mouth and chin exposed. At the back was a single buffalo-horn pointing upward, and under the thongs that fastened it to the mask were thrust numerous green willow branches from above and below, until a great bushy sheaf of them projected above the dancer's head and another swept the ground. Volume V, pages 31-32.

IN THE MEDICINE-LODGE –
ARIKARA, 1908

The Arikara, popularly termed Rees (an abbreviated form of the incorrect spelling, Arickaree), are the northernmost fragment of the Caddoan stock. . . .

In the northward movements the Arikara established their villages at intervals along the Missouri from near the mouth of the Platte to their present locality. . . .

The healers of disease were usually men belonging to the medicine fraternity, but such membership was not essential. In the treatment they used many herbs in connection with the universal incantation; but each herb employed was supposedly possessed of spiritual strength, and the knowledge of its potency with the right to use it was acquired by each medicine-man through revelation, inheritance, or purchase from the other medicine man. . . .

In treating his patient a healer usually remained four days, not singing, but smoking and praying much to his spirit helpers. If no improvement was apparent, he departed and allowed some one else to attempt a cure, but if progress was made under his ministration, he usually remained until the patient could move about. Volume V, pages 59, 64.

AT THE WATER'S EDGE –
PIEGAN, 1910

Since the times of the earliest traditions the buffalo-skin tipi has been used by the Piegan. Volume VI, page 153.

AS IT WAS IN THE OLD DAYS, 1927

In early days, before white men invaded the Great Plains and ruthlessly slaughtered them by hundreds of thousands, bison were of prime importance to the hunting tribes of the vast region in which those animals had their range. The bison was not only the chief source of food of the Plains Indians, but its skin was made into clothing, shields, packs, bags, snowshoes, and tent and boat covers; the horns were fashioned into spoons and drinking vessels; the sinew supplied thread for sewing, bow-strings, and fibre for ropes; the hair was woven into reatas, belts, personal ornaments, and the covers of sacred bundles; and the dried droppings, "buffalo-chips," were used as fuel. So dependent on the buffalo were these Indians that it became sacred to them, and many were the ceremonies performed for the purpose of promoting the increase of the herds. Folio plate 652, Volume XIX.

OFFERING THE BUFFALO-SKULL – MANDAN, 1908

Fasting was observed for the purpose of bringing one's self into communication with the spirits, the suppliant might obtain hopíni, mysterious, power, and thus be enabled to see into the future and to forecast the fate of intended war expeditions. The faster prepared himself by purification in the sweat-lodge and by perfuming his body with sacred sweet-grass; then, clad only in moccasins and loin-cloth, and bearing medicine bundle, buffalo-skull, and pipe, he walked forth alone to some high peak. The start was made very early, since he must reach his goal and be in position when the sun first looked over the edge of the earth. As the sky became illumined by the approaching orb, the suppliant stood on the buffalo-skull and looked to the east, and just as the sun came into view he prayed, "O Sun, give me strength in this deed!" Volume V, page 16.

OGALALA CHILD, 1907

The Lakota, or Teton Sioux, during early historic times occupied the region about Big Stone Lake, in western Minnesota, whence they moved gradually westward, driving the Omaha to the southward and themselves occupying the valleys of the Big Sioux and the James in South Dakota. Making their way still westward, they reached the Missouri, forcing the Arikara southward and penetrating as far as the Black Hills. Volume III, page 3.

ATSINA MAIDEN, 1908

In courting, young men went about in the evening wrapped completely in
buffalo-robes. In asking his sweetheart to marry him, the suitor endeavored
to persuade her to go with him secretly. If she refused, negotiations were
opened between the two families, that of the man taking the initiative. The
value of the gifts offered, and the ability of the young man as a hunter and
warrior, were desiderata. Men under thirty years seldom took wives, for they
were first required to prove their worth in fighting. Volume V, page 154.

A BLACKFOOT TRAVOIS, 1926

The travois is still used for transporting bundles of ceremonial objects.
Before, and sometimes even long after, the acquisition of horses, travoix
were drawn by dogs. Folio plate 637, Volume XVIII.

THE SUN DANCER – APSAROKE, 1908

The Sun Dance, Ashkíshidhuu *(Make Like A Lodge) – not an annual*
performance – was the most spectacular event of the religious calendar. . . .
    The rule was that the dance should not last less than four days
and that the dancer had to remain until he obtained a clear vision.
Sometimes dancers stopped in less than four days, having had their
vision, but this was not often the case. Volume IV, pages 79, 178.

A MEDICINE PIPE – PIEGAN, 1910

Medicine-pipes, of which the Piegan have many, are simply long pipe-stems variously decorated with beads, paint, feathers, and fur. Each one is believed to have been obtained long ago in some supernatural manner, as recounted in a myth. The medicine-pipe is ordinarily concealed in a bundle of wrappings, which are removed only when the sacred object is to be employed in healing sickness, or when it is to be transferred from one custodian to another in exchange for property. Such exchanges, occurring at intervals of a few years in the history of each pipe, are attended by much ceremony. Folio plate 199, Volume VI.

(OPPOSITE)

A GRIZZLY-BEAR BRAVE –
PIEGAN, 1910

At least two of the Piegan warrior societies (the Braves and the All Brave Dogs) included in their membership two men known as Grizzly-bear Braves. It was their duty, at the time of the society dances, to provide their comrades with meat, which they appropriated wherever they could find it. Their expression and demeanor did justice to their name, and in their official capacity they were genuinely feared by the people. Folio plate 198, Volume VI.

(OVERLEAF)

THE BLACKFOOT COUNTRY, 1926

Since the beginning of the historical period the Blackfeet have ranged the prairies along Bow river, while their allies, the Bloods and Piegan, were respectively on Belly and Old Man rivers. In the earliest times of which their traditionists have knowledge the three tribes were respectively on Saskatchewan, Red Deer, and Bow rivers. Folio plate 636, Volume XVIII.

MEDICINE CROW – APSAROKE,
1908

*Born 1846. Mountain Crow; member of the Newly Made Lodge clan
and of the Lumpwood organization. At eighteen he fasted four days
and three nights, and on the morning of the fourth day a spirit
resembling a white man appeared and foretold the passing away of the
buffalo and the coming of many white men with cattle, horses, and
steamboats. His medicine of hawk was purchased from another man.
Counted three first coups, captured five guns and two tethered horses,
and led ten successful war-parties. In a fight with the Nez Percés he
killed a warrior, counted first coup upon him, and captured his gun –
two regular honors at one time, besides the distinction of killing an
enemy. This act he twice repeated in battles with the Arapaho and the
Sioux. Twice he fought on the side of the white men when "their flag
was on the ground": once against the Nez Percés in Chief Joseph's
retreat, and again under General Crook when the Sioux under Sitting
Bull were fleeing across the Canadian border. Medicine Crow
participated in ten severe fights, killed three men, had two horses shot
under him, and had the distinction of having "thrown away" six
wives. Volume IV, page 203.*

*The hawk fastened on the head is illustrative of the manner of wearing
the symbol of one's tutelary spirit. Folio plate 117, Volume IV.*

(OPPOSITE)

OGALALA GIRLS, 1907

As a rule the women of the plains tribes are natural horsewomen, and their skill in riding is scarcely exceeded by that of the men. As mere infants they are tied upon the backs of trusty animals, and thus become accustomed to the long days of journeying. Folio plate 96, Volume III.

(OVERLEAF)

PAINTED LODGES – PIEGAN, 1900

Symbolically painted tipis are frequently observed among the Piegan. Sometimes incidents in the owner's career, especially as a warrior, are depicted, but more often, as in this picture, the painting is conventional, and imitative of a tipi seen by the owner in a vision. Folio plate 186, Volume VI.

DOES EVERYTHING – APSAROKE, 1908

Born 1861. Mountain Crow; Not Mixed clan; Fox organization. When only eighteen or twenty years of age he captured a gun, struck second dákshe, and killed two Piegan in one fight, thus receiving his name. Later he took two horses from the enemy's camp. Volume IV, pages 199-200.

RED PLUME – PIEGAN, 1910

Red Plume describes the camp of his people when he was a youth as a circle a mile or more in diameter and in some places sixteen lodges deep. To have seen such a vast camp would have been worth long privation and hardship.

Their lodges of buffalo-skins, and later of canvas, were of the common tipi form. The testimony of the old men is that they used skin lodges while still in the forest, but this would seem doubtful, particularly as to their winter habitations. They likely began gradually to use them as they moved southward on their hunting expeditions. The one distinctive feature of the Piegan lodges is the characteristic decoration of the inner lining. They, like other Indians, often painted their lodges, so as to indicate either the coups of the owner or his medicine, or sometimes both.

The clothing of the men and women was of the material and pattern usual to the tribes of the northern plains, yet possessing such distinctive marks that one well acquainted with the different tribes could tell almost to a certainty to which one a garment belonged. Volume VI, page 13.

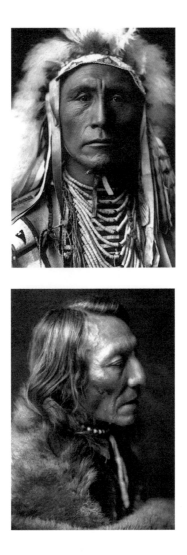

ELK HEAD, AND THE SACRED
PIPE BUNDLE, 1907

According to tradition and the legendary lore of the Teton Sioux, the self-termed Lakota, their teachings — religious, social, ceremonial, and medicinal — are divine laws revealed by . . . White Buffalo Woman, acting as emissary of the Great Mystery. As indicated by their mythology they were, before the coming of this divine messenger, a people with slight knowledge of how to live or to worship. The palladium left with them by White Buffalo Woman was the sacred Calf Pipe, now in the keeping of Elk Head, a member of the Sans Arc band living on the Cheyenne River reservation. . . . He has been the keeper of the pipe for thirty-one years, having received it the year following the Custer fight in 1876. . . .

To the Lakota the pipe is the holy of holies. During the tribal journeying a virgin, carefully guarded by the priest, bore it in advance of the band, and but one instance of the opening of the bundle during Elk Head's priesthood is known. That was when it was taken from him by the Indian police at the command of the resident agent and opened by that official, but the people made such an outcry against the sacrilege that the pipe was quickly restored to its keeper. Volume III, pages 55-56.

A YOUNG HORSEWOMAN, 1908

In the Apsaroke is seen the highest development of the primitive American hunter and warrior. Physically these people were among the finest specimens of their race. They clothed themselves better and dwelt in larger and finer lodges than did their neighbors, and decked their horses in trappings so gorgeous as to arouse the wonder of the early explorers. Volume IV, page xi.

WINTER – APSAROKE, 1908

In the thick forests along the banks of mountain streams the Apsaroke made their winter camps. Folio plate 127, Volume IV.

(OPPOSITE)

PASSING THE CLIFF – APSAROKE, 1908

A winter scene on Pryor creek, Montana. Folio plate 132, Volume IV.

(OVERLEAF)

FOR A WINTER CAMPAIGN – APSAROKE, 1908

It was not uncommon for Apsaroke war-parties, mounted or afoot, to move against the enemy in the depth of winter. . . . The warrior at the left wears the hooded overcoat of heavy blanket material that was generally adopted by the Apsaroke after the arrival of traders among them. The picture was made in a narrow valley among the Pryor mountains, Montana. Folio plate 129, Volume IV.

HIDE STRETCHING –
APSAROKE, 1908

In the camp itself there is an endless panorama of activities and a ceaseless confusion of sounds. Women are everywhere stretching the drying hides, and filling great drying-racks with long thin strips of rich, red buffalo-meat. In the lodges others are tanning skins, and on many sides can be heard the thud of the wooden tray as women gamble with plum-seed dice. Volume IV, page 5.

A HEAVY LOAD – SIOUX, 1908

Summer and winter the Sioux woman performed the heavy work of the camp, and what was seemingly drudgery was to her a part of the pleasure of life. Folio plate 100, Volume III.

LIST OF PLATES

ACKNOWLEDGMENTS

*I would like to acknowledge my profound personal and professional debt to
Edward S. Curtis. Without his extraordinary vision, talents, and commitment, none of this
would be possible. Having had the opportunity to be so intimately involved with his work
has been one of the great joys of my adult life.*

*I would also like to express my sincere gratitude to the many wonderful individuals
at Callaway Editions, Inc. Their commitment to bringing the work of Edward Curtis to
the world involves much hard work. I particularly want to thank my patient and capable
editor Robert Janjigian, as well as Nicholas Callaway, Richard Benson, True Sims,
Jessica Allan, Jennifer Wagner, Daniel Benson, and the many others at Callaway Editions
who played such important roles in making this book a reality.*

*I also wish to thank my assistant Angela Spann for her hard work and many contributions,
and Darren Quintenz and Howard Gottlieb, whose faith in me and whose deep interest in the
work of Edward Curtis have also been instrumental in making all of this possible. — C.C.*

COLOPHON

Great Plains was produced by Callaway Editions, Inc.
70 Bedford Street, New York, NY 10014.
Robert Janjigian, editor. Jennifer Wagner, designer.

Type was composed with Quark Xpress software for Macintosh using a redrawn Franklin
Gothic Extra Condensed typeface and the Centaur typeface from Adobe Systems.

The images selected for this volume were reproduced from an archive of Edward S. Curtis
photographs contained on a CD-ROM. Richard and Daniel Benson converted these
RGB files to a single gray-scale file, from which four printing negatives were generated.
These negatives were printed as quadratones with ink colors that replicate the hues
found in Curtis's original photogravures.

Captions accompanying the Curtis images presented herein are excerpts from Curtis's original
texts found in the twenty volumes and twenty portfolios of The North American
Indian, published from 1907 to 1930, available on CD-ROM through Christopher
Cardozo, Inc., 2419 Lake Place, Minneapolis, MN 55405.

The endpaper design was created using symbols originally printed on the title pages of
volumes I, II, III, IV, V, VII, VIII, X, XII, XIII, XIV, XV, XVIII and XIX of
The North American Indian.

This book was printed and bound by Palace Press International,
Hong Kong, under the supervision of Raoul Goff.